star songs

Composed and compiled by

Joshua Farley

joshfarley2696@gmail.com
Instagram: @wanderlust_wonderlove

table of contents

Prologue………………………………………5

Consciousness Island……………………8

Abuelito Huachuma……………………...10

Flor de la vida……………………………11

Love Your You……………………………12

In the Face of Duality……………………16

Heartsong…………………………………19

The Mandala………………………………20

Stardust……………………………………23

Under a Spell……………………………...25

The Wishing Well that Wishes Well………26

Creative Expression………………………28

Unedited…………………………………...29

Divine Blossoms…………………………..31

Eye of the I………………………………..32

Impermanence……………………………34

Celestially Sweet…………………………35

The Seeker…………………………………36

Site of Insight……………………………...37

Eternal Now………………………………39

Timeless Times………………………………**40**

C'est la vie……………………………………**41**

El mundo en mente…………………………...**43**

Perfect Wisdom………………………………**44**

Living Loving Light…………………………**46**

Starsong………………………………………**48**

The Mage's Handbook………………………**50**

Stop Sign……..………………………………**53**

The We Wheel………………………………..**54**

The Magick Mystique………………………**55**

Malachite……………………………………..**57**

Parallelism……………………………………**61**

½ + ½ = ONE…………………………………**62**

Heart-Filled…………………………………**64**

Dear Universal Creator………………………**65**

Microcosmic………………………………… **67**

Wings of Duality……………………………..**68**

Let Love……………………………………...**70**

Heart Sparks…………………………………**74**

Deep Rest……………………………………**76**

Raindrop Thoughts…………………………...**77**

The Finite Infinite……………………………**79**

You-nity..80

The Wizard's Tower............................82

Instill..86

Sun Island..87

Grow.. 89

Inanimate Animation............................91

The Choice is Yours.............................92

Tout simplement...................................94

Perfection...96

La flor fugaz..97

Morning Prayer....................................98

One Step at a Time..............................100

In the Face of Infinity.........................101

Vaporized.. 104

The Final Act......................................105

prologue

Who am I?

What am I?

"I am on my way,"
is all I can really say.

A spiritual being undergoing a human experience, enamored by the waves of life, love, the light, and the Source thereof.

A spiritual being aligned with the human condition, undergoing the same painstaking processes of the trials and tribulations of our day to day as everyone else.

And, truth be told, I'm okay with that.

So no, I don't know what I am.

I don't know who I am.

And, above all, I don't know *why* I am.

But I do know this: that *I* am. That *you* are. That *we* are. And what I/you/we choose to do with that grain of information is entirely mine/yours/ours alone.

The sky and the stars are singing in you, in me, in us, in every creature and being—animate and inanimate alike—that inhabits our planet, your planet, their planet...

This work is an experiential collection of those *Star Songs* compiled over a three-year span across North America, the tropics and highlands of South America, Europe, and the Caribbean islands. My intention is that you find a sense of peace, clarity, and balance in the verses herein. Though written and revised by my hand alone (with the exception of two), I dare not claim these poems as my own. Rather, they are ours—a wholesome expression of our **Universe** (*uni* = one; *verse* = song).

This collection marks poetry book number three of my present journey on this planet—a synopsis of my learnings and experiences thus far—preceded by *Lucid Reflections*, published in 2020, and *Rainbow Waterfalls*, published in 2021, with many more to come.

I wish to express to you, dear reader, my eternal gratitude for sharing in this illustrious experience of life and delving into my personal perception of the Mind through the letters and locutions contained herein.

Thank you
Gracias
Grazie
Obrigado
Merci
Danke
Takk
Спасибо
Děkuji
Ευχαριστώ

We are all in this together.

consciousness island

I am the creator of my universe
as God is the creator of His,
yet we inhabit the same plane,
                 the same life,
                         the same dream.

As thoughts pervade the mind space,
clouds bind them to consciousness
and storm into the intellect,
subduing being into identification—
a transient spark integrated into
                       untimely
                               reason.

On Consciousness Island,
you are the maker of the daily,
         the waker of the holy,
         the keeper of the deity.

Surrounded by seas of silence
adrift amid illusory sands,
desire leaves you hungry,
passion leaves you weary.

In order not to drown,
the only way **OUT** is **IN**.

As sunrise sows sundown,
the Self reflects within…

The only way out is in…

        The only way out is in…

                The only way out…

- *bird*

abuelito huachuma

I am the energy flowing through the body.
I am the essence that drifts through the Self.

I am the clouds gliding over the mind.
I am the sky that inhabits this space.

I am the rain watering down on Earth's soils.
I am the flowers that gleam in her garden.

I am the jungle absorbed in the Spirit.
I am the eye looking down from above.

— bird

flor de la vida

The flower of life is you,
constantly evolving and
constantly new,
constantly growing and
constantly true,
constantly thriving under
sky shades of blue
with a slight trace of red
just to furnish the hue.

— bird

love your you

Love yourself
like the chickadee
adores the sky;
she doesn't need to ask why,
for her love of the sky is
inherent inside.

Love yourself
like the cardinal
adores her mate;
she doesn't need to ask why,
for her love of her mate is an
immanent trait.

Love yourself
like the mockingbird
adores his song;
he doesn't need to ask why,
for his love of the song is

sublime and lifelong.

Love yourself
like the earthworm
adores the ground;
he doesn't need to ask why,
for his love of the ground is
uniquely earthbound.

Love yourself
like the centipede
adores the tree;
she doesn't need to ask why,
for her love of the tree is
her reason to be.

Love yourself
like the luna moth
adores the night;
she doesn't need to ask why,
for her love of the night is
her soul's divine right.

Love yourself
like the firefly
adores the light;
he doesn't need to ask why,
for his love of the light
is embedded in flight.

Love yourself
like the grizzly bear
adores the air;
she doesn't need to ask why,
for her love of the air is
the cub of her care.

Love yourself
like the arctic hare
adores the grass;
he doesn't need to ask why,
for his love of the grass is
his reason days pass.

Love yourself
like the wild flower
adores the sun;
she doesn't need to ask why,
for her love of the sun is
what makes her feel **ONE**.

Love yourself
like the pygmy owl
adores the moon;
he doesn't need to ask why,
for his love of the moon is
the source of his tune.

Love yourself
like I love you,
for to love yourself is
to live life true,
and truth be told…
well…
there is no **WE** if there is no **YOU**.

- bird

in the face of duality

The soul resides in the darkest corners
where polarities intertwine,

For, you see,
opposites attract…

The left and right merge,
forming a single hand
by which the light of thought,
through transmutation toward intention,
finds its freedom in mindful expression.

Pour black paint over white
and you'll find the formation of
nothing new,
but rather
more → just → same;
↳ of ↲ ↳ the ↲

the same color,
a varied context,
a new light,
an angle shifted.

We inhabit a cosmic soup of creative flavors
where colors cast contrast o'er canvas of white
overlaid with black—
two versions of the same
ONE.

Where duality may arise,
black becomes white and
white becomes black and
gray becomes green and
salt becomes sweet,
fire is ice and
love is hate,
old is new and
the lies of late become true.

I am I but
I am U and
x is y when
LOVE is true…

Which must be true,
for the *is-ness* of this is…

The outcome…
of this…   and that…
and there…   and back…
now and then…   where and when…

A fine line in a seam of time where the
why
and the   *how*
and the   *who*
are elements of the same story,
all of which…
are manifest…
by **YOU**.

- bird

heartsong

The inner child begs forgiveness
for the sins he can't recall,
as the elders sing with sacred wealth
the songs the plants resolve.

The heart, it shifts,
it shapes and lifts,
as darkness sheds
and light embeds.

Truth recalls the inner sight
and soaks the soul
in heart-fueled might.

Your freedom is your *Self*,
your noble path,
you sun-sought wealth;

community does bind us all
to rise above
                the shadow's call.

The dark night of the soul,
it withers with the rising sun,
whence we all shall shine together,
divinely lit,
becoming
ONE.

— bird

the mandala

I am not my body…
I am not my mind…
I am merely **ONE**
with the infinite divine.

I am energetic subtlety
seeking simple solace
solely for the
silent soul.

I am the subtle stillness
that silence sings
as suns soar over
spacious strings.

I am I and I,
which means you and me
and them and we,
don't you see?

For we are not our bodies…

and we are not our minds…

we are merely **ONE**

with the infinite design.

— bird

life's first song

In darkness vast where stars are born,
from cosmic dust in light's first form,
hydrogen fused in stellar fire,
a burst of life—boundless desire.

Through eon's drift in space so wide,
the remnants of those stars collide.
Dust and force by gravity's hand
craft the Earth, the seas and sand.

From stardust rich in cosmic grace,
life took root, began to trace
molecules in river flows—
breathing sparks that sprung life's glow.

Now here we stand—a living song—
particles where stars belong.

Each beat of heart, each breath we take,
a starlit memory, in glimpse, awakes.

Each beat of heart, each breath we take,
a starlit memory, in glimpse, awaits.

— vibe

under a spell

Love is my natural state.

Joy is my natural state.

Abundance is my natural state.

Peace is my natural state.

This is my harmony,
the way I must be,
undisturbed and unrestrained,
unperturbed and unexplained;
under the spell of the witful domain;
under the well of the life-bearing rain.

- bird

the wishing well that wishes well

The darkest nights of the soul spring forth
the brightest incantations:
treasure troves inlaid with gold,
grimoires lined with spells untold.

Trust in the unfailing compass of
the ever-soaring spirit
which leads the lost to oneness
through paths sublime and shunless.

Your spellcraft sings the softest hymns of
consciousness rehearsed within;
may the charm your magick brings
grant your soul with lasting wings.

Stay the noise,
seek your voice,
be the seer
of all life's joys.

Cast your spell,
write your tale,
then revel in
the wishing well.

- bird

Creative Expression

Creativity is
The key to infinity
A gift of divinity
A heart-filled affinity
The path to serenity

Creativity is
Infinity is
Divinity is
Affinity is
Serenity is
Creativity

— bird

unedited

My mind seeks a sweet escape
like syllables seeping from a singer's soul
or written on a whim
on the very first go…

No edits…
    No revisions…
        No critiques…

The words just <u>flow</u>.

The seasons, they come,
my worries, they know,
they have no
destination to go.

No sights to see…
    No where to be…
        No lies to believe…

Just a gentle breeze
off the open seas
to bring the Self
to soulful ease.

So breathe…

    No, really,
        just breathe.

Your agenda is imaginary,
your destination—stationary.

You have nowhere to be
but the place you feel
most   free.

So please, just breathe…

        Let it be
        AND
        Let it flee.

-

divine blossoms

May you flower

May you shine

May you live your light

DIVINE

- bird

eye of the i

I weave infinity
through awareness
of the mind's eye;
well, not I,
but the eye
of the midnight sky.

But is it I?
Or is it the eye
which I spy
in the midnight sky?

A reflection looking back,
a mirror in reverse;
the eye of the mind
by the universe designed
staring back

from the eye
of the I
which I perceive like stars
in the midnight sky.

*"No creo nunca haber visto
tantas estrellas a la vez."*

- bird

impermanence

Whereas impermanence is at
the root of all things,
unwillingness to change becomes
the root of dis-ease.

To be attached to the mind
and the sorrow it brings
is to forego the default modes
of joy, love, and peace.

— bird

celestially sweet

Do not reject the divine pleasures of life
but hold them dear in your heart ♥ filled hands,
for they are sweet of soul
and sneer not at the sight of your light.

Existence—a gift,
persistence—a choice;
let your cheer be upheld
by the grace of the voice;
not the voice of the body
nor the jeering of mind,
but the voice of the
wholesome
enlightened
DIVINE.

— bird

the seeker

Seek the stars in the sky at night;
become aware of your self-insight.
                    [your Self in sight]

Seek the start of a thought in flight;
see that it's naught but a flicker of light.

Seek the second you spot a new sight;
see it's a moment that's frozen alight.

Seek the difference between black and white;
see they're the same,
just an altered skylight.

Seek the feeling when nations unite;
see the answer to a meaningless fight.

Seek in the eyes of a good friend
to see past the eyes of a good friend—

past the disguise so slyly concealed
by their suit and their ties.

Seek your calm under dim candlelight;
tranquil and soft—
a green halophyte.

Seek your soul in the din of twilight;
merge with the Spirit as planets unite.

Seek…
    and seek…
        and seek…
            and seek…

For the One is to be sought
in the timeless mystique.

- bird

site of insight

The site of insight is seeded in stillness,
in spite of the sight of the slighting of shrillness.

The willingness,
the motionless,
the fearless
and speechless,
all manifest
for the sake of
the oneness,
of mindfulness
and service
to the practice of justice
and the skyward flow
of our flawless forgiveness.

- bird

eternal now

For as long as the universe has existed,

there has only ever been

one

single

moment…

→ NOW ←
(with arrows from above and below)

— bird

timeless times

When you leave behind time
and bathe in the now,
you'll find that your time
is worth less than a dime

              ... worthless.

           THEN,

When you learn to
~~~~~**enjoy**~~~~~
the passage of time,
you'll be gifted a key,
the treasure of which
will make you so rich
you'll never again
ask for dimes
based on time. / =)

- bird

c'est la vie

It's your life,
and you get to pick.

You can pick money…
but you don't have to.

You can pick fame…
but you don't have to.

You can pick comfort…
but you don't have to.

You can pick nationalism…
but you don't have to.

You can pick religion…
but you don't have to.

You can pick love…
but you don't have to.

You can pick life…
but you don't have to.

Because, you see,
it's your life…
and you get to pick.

- bird

el mundo en mente

Eres la perfección de Dios,
tus ojos la reflexión de los ríos…

Con el mundo en mente
y el cariño presente,
me cautivas siempre;
una sonrisa permanente.

- bird

perfect wisdom

Perfect wisdom is in my heart,
infinite knowledge within my reach.
To view each day as a work of art,
o, won't Mother Nature take over and teach?

O, teach me the difference
between the soul and the sky,
or the intricate nature
of the Self and the I.

Delve deep in the demons
that dwell in my night
and where they may go
on the day that I die.

I seek and I seek
for the things I can't see.
I seek and I seek
in this world 'round me.

But the more that I seek
the more that I find
there's a yearning within
which can't be defined;
a yearning for questions
which puzzle the mind
and will not be answered
by your gods nor mine.

We yearn for mystery
   ... for dialogue
      ... for history;
but if truth be told,
what's hidden is the master key...

Perfect wisdom is in my heart,
infinite knowledge within my reach.
To view each day as a work of art,
o, won't Father Divine take over and teach?

- bird

living loving light

If you had the world in the palm of your hands,
would you know what to do with it?

Would you rattle and shake it
then fumble and break it?
Or humbly take it
and spiritually wake it?

How you live your life
is your message
to the world.

Live it with love.
Live it with light.
Lease it new air and
breathe it new life.

For how you love your light

is your message

to the world.

- bird

starsong

You are my soul's best friend
    my guiding hand
    the feeling of sand
    as my feet sink deep
    in your love-fertile land

You are my animate night
    my path to the light
    my sky-seeking sight
    as my hands bear down
    on these words that I write.

You are my compass at sea
    my reason to be
    the fruit-bearing tree
    that nurtures my veins
    and sets my song free.

You are **LOVE**   You are **LIGHT**

You are **SOUND**   You are **SIGHT**

You are **INNER**   You are **OUTER**

You are **DAY**   You are **NIGHT**

You are the stars that dance bright

as they sing through the night

and the moons which gift might

to our orbits alike.

- bird

the mage's handbook

1) Be watchful of that
   which you do or you say,
   for the reality of magick
   is always at play.

2) As you wander the path,
   stay aware of the Self,
   for the knowledge of Self
   is the path to true wealth.

3) To predict the future
   one has to create it,
   for your word is your will
   And you mustn't forsake it.

4) Hold true to your Self,
   your intentions and quirks,
   for soon you will behold
   the fruit of your works.

5) Stay a student of life
through age and decay,
for to flow with the world
is to seize each new day.

6) Realize you don't know
and say not a word,
for through nurture of mind
will you clearly be heard.

7) View Divinity in Nature
and Earth as Divine,
for it's in every creature,
every place, every time.

8) Be clear with intention—
what your inner eyes see—
for the strength of your will
is your will to be free.

9) Make magick your artform—
   your science of faith—
   for each intuition's
   but a riddle engaged.

10) Hold open your heart
    to the breathing design,
    for embedded in All
    is the lawful lifeline.

11) Know the creatures as companions,
    the flora as your friends,
    for the Earth shall hold harmless
    all those who make amends.

    May your magick carry through;
    may your blessings all come true;
    may your words form something new
    as our planet cradles you.

- bird

stop sign

The moment you stop trying to be someone
is the moment you realize
you don't have to run.

So stop trying to be someone
and just be **ONE**.

– bird

the we wheel

Without — **YOU**
There is no — **ME**
And without — **ME**
There is no — **WE**

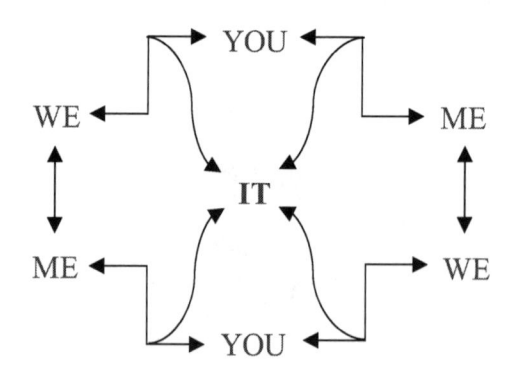

```
          YOU
           ↓
  WE ←         → ME
   ↕     IT      ↕
  ME ←         → WE
           ↑
          YOU
```

... what's the difference?

— *bird*

the magick mystique

Magick is science undiscovered.
Magick is silence under the cover.

Magick is speaking your truth like a lover
bound to her word with no space for another.

Magick is formless,
yet forms shapes and sound.

Magick's the inner
and outer abound.

Magick's the figure
looking back from the mirror.

Magick's the hearer
of our voice ringing clearer.

Magick's infinity,
encompassing **YOU**.

Magick's the sinner,
mistaken and skew.

~~*~*~*~*~*~*~*~*~*~*~*~*~*~*~*

May your words cast your spells
and your actions your tales;
when the intellect fails,
intuition prevails.

- bird

malachite

I walk with the knowledge I am
safe and **protected**.

I pray with awareness I am
whole and **connected**.

I seek for the oneness I
know is **embedded**
in the hearth of the Spirit so
calm and **collected**.

I sing under raindrops so
light and **life-bearing**.

I stand under treetops so
shrewd and **shade-sharing**.

I water the life-crops so **wholesome** and **daring** to enliven my cells with the **kindness** of **caring**.

I am whole,
I am here,
I am **conscious** of **home**.

I am one with the realms of the **skylight** and **throne**.

I have heard of the songs of the **poets** of **Rome** who pleaded and prayed to the **depths** so **unknown**.

I'm open to the prowess of **healing** and **love**.

I'm grateful to the Dreamer who
dreams from **above**.

I'm as blessed for this life and the
One **Mind** **thereof**
as I'm blessed for the song of the
dawn's **mourning** **dove**.

May this gift of awareness bring us
long - **lasting** **peace**.

May this wondrous knowledge bring our
love to **increase**.

May this eternal life teach us
all to **release**
from the chains and the shackles of a
life - **binding** **lease**.

      I'm blessed for existence
      and
      I'm blessed for your time.

I'm blessed for this life

and

the gift of our rhyme.

- bird

parallelism

Merge with the forces
of the forest thereat,
for there is no distinction
in the *this* and the *that*.

- bird

½ + ½ = 𝑜𝑛𝑒

What if you lost your soul today?

Where would you be?
What would you be?
And most importantly,
why would you be?

Your existence would be non-existence,
your essence
evanescence,
your effervescence
efflorescence.

In the light of the Source of the One,
the light would cease to be light;
harmony at once would seem to unite
with the voidness and blankness
of bearing no sight,
and the only thing left…

The only thing left would be right,
and all which was right would be left.

Duality—
two halves of the One:
fire and ice,
evil and nice,
friendship and war,
nothing and more;
separated solely by the
scales of synchronicity.

- bird

heart-filled

I am overfilled with gratitude

on this day,

or heart ♥ filled with grace,

as one might say,

for another breath of life

has come my way,

another day to dream,

come whatever may.

— bird

dear universal creator

I am profoundly grateful for
this chance to experience:
> the manifest world
> the joy of our life
> the landscape unending
> the grace of the light
> the cheer of our dance
> the voices inside
> the realm of our dreams
> the beauty of sight
> the songs of the birds
> the void of the mind
> the essence to **BE**
> the feeling of might
> the soundwaves of song
> the clash of our plight
> the gifts of creation

the creative insight

the fellowship of love

the cat's loving bite

the fruits of the Earth

the bright of sunlight

the sharing of nature

the poems we write

the taste of a pear

the calm of twilight

the power of now

the stars set alight

the kingdom of sky

the darkness of night

the solace of sleep

the flit of candlelight

the sipping of tea

the call of starlight

the stillness of silence

the taste of midnight

the wholesome embrace

of our holy birthright

- bird

microcosmic

A good meditation session
> is but a microcosm
>> of a life well-lived.

- bird

wings of duality

Contemplation and stillness are
two wings of the same bird—
the grand condor seeking solace
atop the deep Colca precipice,
its plumage rustling in harmony
as the shaman chants upon its grace.

The body and mind are
two wings of the same bird—
the Canada goose alongside its flock,
soaring as **ONE** underneath the sky-clock,
counting aimlessly from infinity
unto creation's initial singularity.

Love and hate—	Will and fate—
the cardinals	the parrots
of emotion.	of vibration.

Black and white—
the chickadees
of perception.

Day and night—
the magpies
of creation.

One is all and
    all is sewn,
    all's okay
when love is known.

May all shout loud
to the unknown:
"I have arrived.
  I have come home."

- bird

let love

Close your eyes,
open your heart,
feel the emanation spring from within…

Is it warm?
What color is your love?
And did you notice…?

Keep them closed just a little bit harder,
hold that feeling just a little bit longer,
and then you'll see…
it just isn't ending;
it just keeps on flowing…

The love pouring from your center
is infinite,
eternal…

See,

you have no limitation;

a limitless being in

a limited world;

a limitless creation

of manifestation.

That makes you capable of quite a lot,

to be sure…

So let love leak to those around,

for all life is worthy,

all beings deserving,

and truth be told,

you'll never run out—

not out of love,

that is.

Empty your vessel,

the ground will refill.

Empty your mental,
the sky will reveal.

Drain your love,
the divine will rain down
with oceans
and oceans   ***ABOUND***.
and oceans

Abundance is your natural state
when sharing stays an open plate.

Now,
I'll tell you a dark truth,
at first it may hurt…
in fact, it may hurt a lot.

But fear not, my friend,
for sweet is the taste
and the feeling unique;
but still, in the end,
the reward's not what we seek.

So LET *LOVE* free.

So LET *LOVE* flee.

So LET *LOVE* lead

so that

    LOVE may be.

- bird

heart sparks

Think about the moment you have a thought—
the light of a frequency in motion that's caught…

Observe that instance
if just for an instant,
for instantly it turns
a distant   existence
of persistent   intermittence…

Or so I thought…
until intention was sought
by the thought of said thought
to be brought into action
and tied in a knot
to the fabric of reaction,
tau(gh)t in accordance
with the concordance of
manifestation—

the action of intention

        in reaction to

                thoughtful

                        intuition.

                            - bird

deep rest

To be depressed
is not
giving up,
sacrificing your will,
or denying your skill;

To be depressed
is to
seek deep rest,
putting your mask to bed
and living your truth instead.

— bird

raindrop thoughts

To lessen your pace to the rhythm of plants
is to sway with the wind
with no qualms,
with no plans.

Rather than raindrops falling up high
like intricate thoughts in a restless old mind,
let yourself tumble toward the sunshine—
the full cosmic flow of the final divine.

The trees do speak,
yet you move so quick,
and the flowers do heal
when your spirit does kneel.

Revere the ground
as your worship the sky,
for above is below
like reflections aligned.

So when time does come
for your healing inside,
seek not to run
but solely to hide
from the world outside
where temptations reside
and the nature of mind
which seeks to deride.

So sit with the moss
and a rose by your side
and breathe with the trees
as they gently reside.

- bird

the finite infinite

The gift of our *finite* time
paired with the promise of
        in*finite* potential
may constitute the greatest of all life's sufferings,
for it is within this duality
that we fall into the maze of the
                      minutes
                            of
                                time.

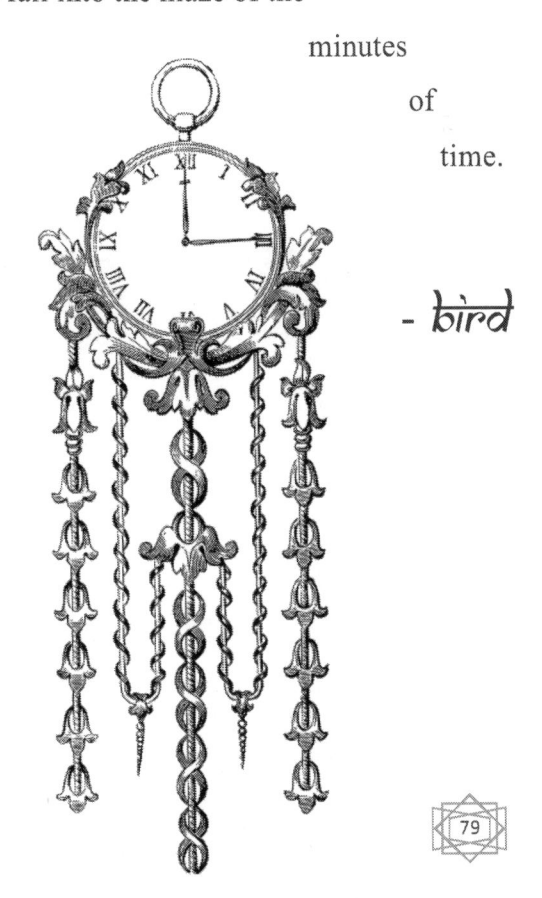

                          - bird

you-nity

Earth is the artist,
we are the brushes,
land is the canvas
for imagination boundless.

So go where the love is;
so pray with the hopeless;
so paint with the goddess
to share with the loveless.

Not for the selfish and
not for the selfless,
but for the sole purpose
of living the oneness,
of living the kindness,
of living the wholeness,
of living the why-ness;
of living the you-nity and
living the I-nity

from the eternal now

to the bounds of infinity.

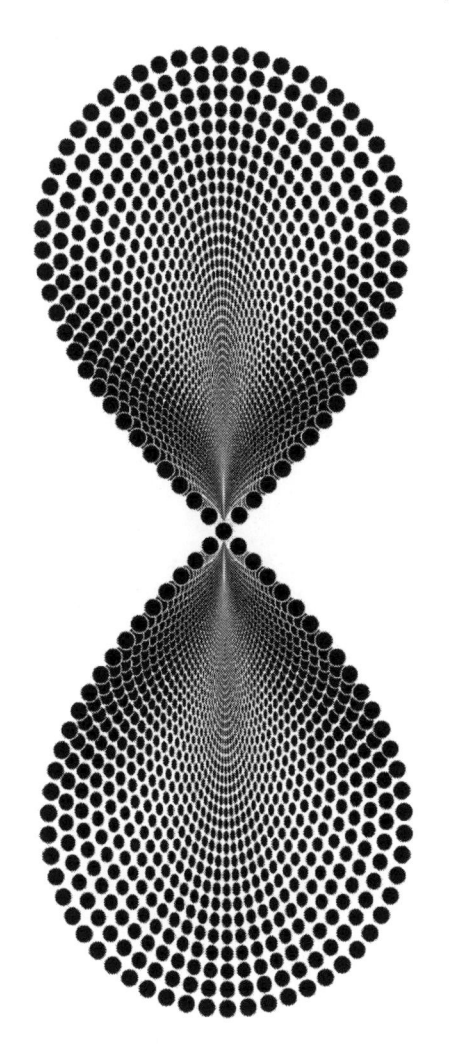

- ~~bird~~

the wizard's tower

Whitewashed walls
wither the will
of wayfaring wanderers
worried and ill
while wicked weavers
work to instill
their weathering wrath—
a wintering chill.

Whereas wise wizards
willfully write,
their witherless words
warring off wicked might,
so do waxwings and warblers
wail with the light
with weasels and whales
'til wheeled off by night.

Wonderfully whimsically
weaving with spirit,
the white wizard warmfully
writes of a secret
to ward off the warring
and wrathfully wicked,
then warily hears
welcome knocks at his wicket.

The witch of the west
does arrive with a wicker
woven from willow
with woodruff and pepper,
wairakite, wavellite,
wiluite, copper,
and worthwhile wares
to ward off the ripper.

"Why, welcome white witch
to my walloping tower
which wobbles and waves
with the weight of each hour;

wanton and wild
do the wicked deflower
the wayfaring wanderers
now withdrawn of power;
would that words of wisdom
water the flower
and waken the Wise Ones
that wield all willpower."

"What words would accomplish,"
the white witch did wail,
"would work with the wondrous
wits of a spell,
and whereas your words
are written so well
and my withstanding herbs
will willfully pair,
may we work with the wisdom
thus woven by air
to wither the wicked
and weave loving care."

So wizard and witch
did work with the Wise
who walk with the winged
and wander the skies
'til the wicked were wrung out
with words of demise
and ripped from the worlds
on which they wrought lies.

Such is the tale
of the witch and the wizard
who withheld the wrathful
and wintering blizzard.

- bird

instill

Stay still like the lake
when the breeze starts to cease;
stay calm like the stones
at their ease by the seas;
stay centered and focus
like the bees in their trees
as they buzz without fuss
as their home hive decrees.

Find oneness in stillness
and stillness at once
through the calm core of kindness
instilled by the One.

— bird

sun island

La isla del sol—
the seat of my soul—
the sole place I know
where my song can sing slow.

In the midst of the lake
where my heart's most awake,
I pray for the sake
of the dawn of daybreak.

I pray for the joy
and the comfort of all.

I pray for the sun,
may it rise and it fall.

I pray for the love
of creation to call

on the angels above,

may they crumble this wall,

such to unveil the oneness—

        the oneness of all—

and awaken our hope

through the crane's sweetened call.

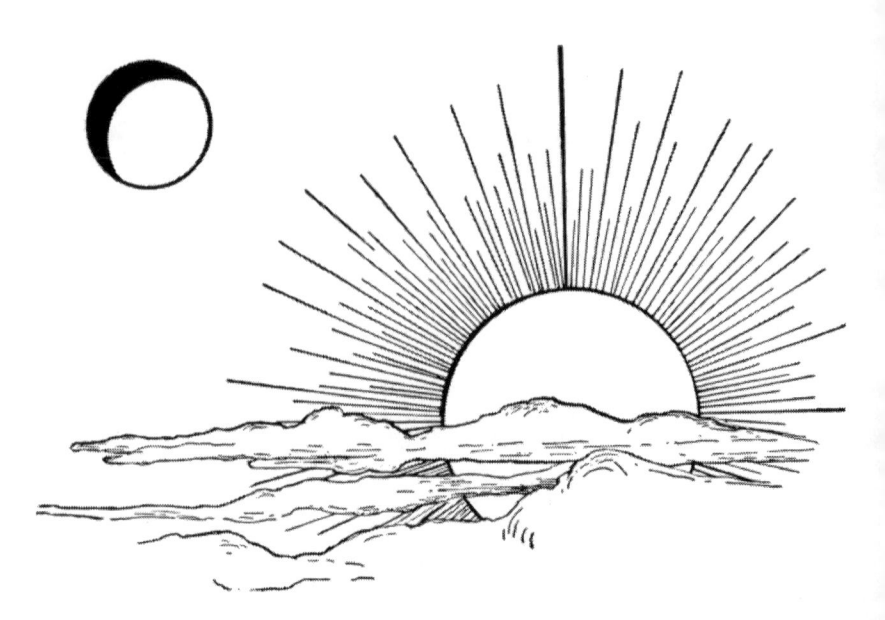

- bird

grow

To grow you must let go,
like trees release their brittle leaves
or leaves flow down Earth's gentle streams.

To grow you must let go,
like dark clouds break on stormy days
or flowers dream their nights away.

To grow you must let go,
like baby birds that leave their nest,
now on their own, they'll fly their best.

To grow you must let go,
like the whale's young calf now out at sea,
a whole wide world now out to see.

To grow,
you must let go.

— star

inanimate animation

If mountains had wings,
I think they would stay
right where they are,
content with their place in this space
where the sun and the stars
never cease to align.

~~~~~~~~~~~AND~~~~~~~~~~~

If oceans had legs,
I think they would end up
right where they start,
content with their seat at the feet
of where rivers and streams
never cease to combine.

- bird

the choice is yours

Love is not something you do,
it's something you are.

Compassion is not something you give,
it's something you are.

Joy is not something you feel,
it's something you are.

In the light of hate,
embody love,
for they're mirror images
of the same spectral form.

In the light of dejection,
embody compassion,
for they're mirror images
of the same spectral form.

In the light of misery,

embody joy,

for they're mirror images

of the same spectral form.

But, hey,

THE CHOICE IS YOURS. =)

- bird

tout simplement

The more that I grow,
the more that I realize
I'm not interested in making a living…

But simply in living…

But simply in loving…

But simply in sharing
this life with the daring,
and simply in bearing
more fruits for the caring…

May we share all our meals,
may we share all these hills,
may we shed these ideas
of laws, lands, and bills.

This land—it is *ours*,
neither yours, neither mine;
it thrives for all plants
and all species alike.

So care for the Earth
and your neighbors abound
and you'll find that the seas
sing a simpler sound.

- bird

perfection

The *perfection* of creation
is a *perfection* attained through
imperfection.

— *bird*

la flor fugaz

En la soledad
encuentro la paz,
que en nuestra era
nos puede parecer
algo fugaz.

Algo detrás de
lo que solemos buscar
en el mar de la mente;

Algo fugaz que
nos puede parecer
la flor de la paz.

— bird

morning prayer

Dear Universal Creator,
Pachamama,
fellow guardians,
and dearest Starya:

I am profoundly grateful
for another day on Earth,
another chance to experience
life and creativity
and to share in the boundlessness
of the emanating Source.

May all beings on this day encounter
peace, love, and joy;
may Spirit grow ever-wider
as more advance on the path of light,
like a butterfly effect in infinite flight
or flowers breathing an endless spring.

Thank you for this giving of living
and all of the beings with whom
I'm existing.

I look forward to the merging with the light
on my merry way back home,
but until then,
I'll anticipate with joy
every
lasting
waking
moment.

Gracias.

- bird

one step at a time

When your mind rushes outward,
    just step in and breathe.

When your thoughts turn to puzzles,
    just step back and see.

When your senses are heated,
    just step toward the breeze.

When you lose your true Self,
    just step out and be.

Don't let your frustrations become what you see
nor surrender the insight that lets you be free,
for intentions are waves in your spell-binding sea
that water the roots of your life-bearing tree.

- bird

in the face of infinity

The infinite is right in front of you
all the time...
in awe divine...

The timeless trees tower
tremendously o'er the litters of leaves
they leave behind.

The clouds of cotton cake
cast overhead
cross the cosmos
collectively and quizzically
in constant contemplation of the
sounding seas which surf
surreptitiously
from side to side
as the birds below
browse at the bountiful abundance wherein
borders becomes boundless bridges

boasting their beauty in balance

with the breath-filled elements abound.

The infinite is

aimless and endless,

outward and inward,

forever deviating,

        yet always

  on   the

PATH.

The infinite is.

The infinite was.

The infinite will.

Forever a timeless presence both

lost and found,

here and there,

then and now,

free and bound.

Its non-existence is the reason it exists.

- ~~bird~~

vaporized

Without the story,
there is no dream;
this dream of life
being what I mean.

By day we share
in the linear stream,
yet by night does it rise—
a vapor of steam;
a brand-new seam
woven in the tapestry
of our everlastful dream…

This dream of life
being what I mean.

— *bird*

the final act

The theater of consciousness:
a play of the soul,
a play of the Source
where we all play a role;
a play of the part that's
a part of the whole;
a play in which time's
but a word on a scroll.

May the poets still sing,
may their stories still thrive,
on this stageplay of life
where the props come alive.

— bird

Made in the USA
Columbia, SC
06 January 2025